Pubs of Wimbledon Town
(Past & Present)

by

Clive Whichelow

Published by

Enigma Publishing

4 Charnwood Avenue

London SW19 3EJ

First edition September 2021

ISBN 978-0-9524297-9-1

Printed by Aquatint

CONTENTS

INTRODUCTION

So where is 'Wimbledon town'? For the purposes of this book it is the area covered by the old parish of Wimbledon – apart from Wimbledon Village, the pubs of which have been covered in a previous book.

Many of the pubs of 'Wimbledon town' were not in the centre, but on the outskirts, particularly towards the eastern boundary of the parish in and around Haydon's Road.

In the early 19th century 'Wimbledon' meant just what we now call Wimbledon Village. There was very little housing 'down the hill' until the coming of the railway in 1838. Even then, the building of 'New Wimbledon' or 'South Wimbledon' was slow and by the time of the 1861 census there were only a thousand people living south of the railway. Within ten years though this was to quadruple and by 1881 the figure was 8000. As soon as the population increased so did the number of pubs.

There were one or two inns outside the village before the railway came though. In Plough Lane was the Plough inn which had been there since at least 1721 and in Merton High Street, next to what is now the bus garage, was the Kings Head. This was there from about 1725, though it claimed a much earlier date. After this came the Horse and Groom in Haydon's Road and the Mansel Tavern (later the South Western Hotel) just opposite Wimbledon station.

The reason two of the pubs were there was because the King's Head was on the main coaching route into London and the Mansel Tavern served the users of the new railway station. Later pubs appeared in the areas where the new housing was built – e.g. in and around Haydon's Road. These modest dwellings would have been ideal for railway workers, builders, and other tradesmen. Indeed, the names of some of the pubs show who they were trying to appeal to, for example, The Plasterers Arms and The Joiners Arms. In fact, some of the pubs were run by men who had other trades and occupations.

As the area south of the railway expanded the number of pubs increased accordingly and a few years after they had appeared in and around Haydon's Road they started to pop up in Wimbledon Broadway and Kingston Road too. This continued into the 1880s and then there was a gap of a hundred years before a spate of new pubs opened up in the 1990s.

Sadly, in recent years, the number of pubs in Wimbledon has declined and some much-loved old locals have gone. The Broadway Tavern (formerly the Freeman Arms) in Wimbledon Broadway has closed as has the King's Head in Merton High Street. In Haydon's Road we have lost the British Queen and the Marquis of Lorne, and in Plough Lane the Plough inn that gave the road its name. Several others have gone too, even including some of the more recent additions from the 1990s.

Some, happily, seem to be thriving: the Alexandra at the bottom of Wimbledon Hill, the Prince of Wales opposite the station, and the Sultan in Norman Road. The Horse and Groom in Haydon's Road survives as The Garden Shed, and the Woodman at Wimbledon Park reopened in 2019 after fears that it would be knocked down following its closure in 2017.

But over the years there have been many other pubs that have been and gone and quite often their stories, and even their very existences have been forgotten so it seems time for them to be remembered.

So, pour yourself a drink and take an armchair 'walk' around the pubs of Wimbledon town.

WAS WIMBLEDON BUILT ON BEER?

It seems that when Wimbledon town (i.e. the area outside Wimbledon Village) was being built some of the earliest buildings were pubs or beer houses. As the first houses were built in and around Haydon's Road from the 1850s onwards so the number of pubs and beer houses increased. Some were clearly aimed at the artisans who were to build subsequent houses and as the number of houses increased so did the number of drinking establishments. By the 1880s there were nine pubs in or just off Haydon's Road, not including nearby ones such as the Woodman in Durnsford Road or the King's Head and Royal Six Bells in Merton High Street.

A note on history: people tend to think of 'history' as being about what happened in the past. It is really though only about what is recorded, and the truth is that a lot of things have never been recorded. We sometimes find brief mentions of pubs that once existed locally but no other details, and even more commonly, no photographs. This book therefore attempts to present as much interesting information as possible about the pubs but is limited to the facts available at time of writing.

PRESENT PUBS (19TH CENTURY ORIGIN)

Considering the number of pubs that were once in Wimbledon it is perhaps shocking that there are only half a dozen of the 19th century ones left.

It is sadly the same story in Merton and Mitcham (which has lost around half of its pubs), as it is elsewhere. Even some of the Wimbledon town pubs that remain have been threatened with closure in recent years but have managed to keep going by diversifying what they offer and also by the support and protests of regular drinkers.

The 19th century pubs are really quite a different thing from the modern pubs as in the Victorian era they were not just drinking places but also venues for sales, inquests, meetings etc. They could sometimes even be used as virtual A&E departments in the days before we had a hospital in Wimbledon. They were therefore a much more integral part of the civic community than the 20th century ones and much local history is connected with them.

In fact, it is probably no exaggeration to say that, along with the churches, pubs were at the centre of the community. Political meetings were held there, trades union meetings, property auctions, entertainments, and in the grounds of the pubs were sporting events, garden parties, and more. Before Wimbledon town was properly developed some of these pubs had a substantial amount of land, and in many cases, were surrounded by fields.

Pub landlords were respected members of the community, and in Wimbledon Village, before the town developed, they had often sat on the vestry committee which decided matters of the parish, such as welfare of the poor, upkeep of the roads, building of civic amenities, law and order, etc. As the 19th century went on their role was less important as the local government district of Wimbledon began in 1866 and the first town hall was built in 1878.

So to begin with, let's look at the remaining pubs that have their roots in early Wimbledon town.

ALEXANDRA

This impressive town centre pub at the bottom of Wimbledon Hill was here by 1868 and the first we hear of it is in November of that year when details of the candidates in the Mid-Surrey elections could be obtained here as well as at other pubs in Battersea, Wandsworth, Richmond and Reigate etc. It is surprising that the honour wasn't given to the nearby Mansel Arms which had been established much longer. To begin with, the pub was known as the Alexandra Tavern and the owner in 1868 was John Andrews. The road at the side then was Grove Road before it became St Mark's Place.

In 1871 the pub was sold, along with four houses at the rear. It was said to be doing a 'large trade in malt liquors but capable of considerable extension'. It was also said to have had stables.

By 1873 the landlord, George Smith was applying for a new licence to sell 'spirits, wine, beer, porter, cider, perry and other intoxicating liquors'. He held the pub on a 75-year lease.

Whoever owned the land also owned other land nearby as in 1875 an advert in the Surrey Comet was offering building land on the area adjacent to the pub for the erection of shops, villas and cottages.

As with other local pubs, inquests were held here. In March 1881 the body of a young woman by the name of Elizabeth Gilpen had been found drowned in the Rushmere pond on Wimbledon Common. It was heard that the 35-year-old servant had been suffering from depression, fearing that she may have to go to the workhouse when her husband died and her employer decided to terminate her position. The poor, desperate woman had even had to break the ice on the pond in order to drown herself. Her body was found by a local vicar, Rev Bernard Reynolds.

A couple of days earlier an 80-year-old retired railwayman was killed crossing the railway line just outside the station. The inquest was told that the man was hard of hearing and did not hear the warning whistle of the Southampton express train.

In 1885 an inquest heard that a 15-year-old errand boy was decapitated after laying his head over the tracks at Wimbledon since losing his job and allegedly being threatened by his stepmother that she would not give him food or clothing if he failed to find another one. Inquests here were often in connection with people who had been involved in accidents on the railway at Wimbledon.

The licensing laws in the late nineteenth century were yet to be as restrictive as they would become a few decades later. In May 1894 a Wimbledon gardener was up before the magistrates for being 'drunk and incapable' in St Mark's Place outside the Alexandra. Nothing unusual in that you might think, but this was when he'd just come out of the pub at nine o'clock in the morning! The policeman who found him, appropriately named PC Constable, said the man was lying on the pavement 'helplessly drunk', though the accused claimed to have been in the Alexandra for just half an hour. Before the First World War pubs could open at 6.00 am. The gardener was given a choice of a 10 shilling fine or seven days in jail.

But 'The Alex' had its happier associations too. The Wimbledon News reported in April 1900 that the pub was the venue for the annual dinner of The Wimbledon Piscatorial Society, an event at which the walls were festooned with examples of fish such as chub, carp, bream and tench that had been caught by members. It was reported that the dinner was a great success but does not say if fish was on the menu.

An advertisement in the Surrey Independent in 1898 shows the pub as The Alexandra Hotel and offers rooms to let for concerts, clubs and committee meetings. It also offered hot and cold luncheons and billiards. Local newspaper ads show that trades union meetings were held here as well as property auctions, meetings of the Hearts of Oak Benefit Society, etc. In 1885 it was also the venue for the first annual dinner of the Wimbledon & District Licensed Victuallers Protection Society. In this period there was a strong temperance movement, with the Wimbledon branch of the Church of England Temperance Society forming in 1877 so local publicans probably felt they needed their own society to stand up for their interests. They pointed out that they paid a fifth of all taxation in the country.

Although by the end of the 19th century pubs such as the Alexandra seemed to be moving into the modern world, just a few years previously, in 1883, a woman living next door died from suspected cholera and the doctor who attended attributed the infection to 'the stench arising from the accumulation of stable manure in the space between the hotel and the house.' The local board (forerunner to the council) however was not satisfied that the infection was cholera, and did not record it as such, not wishing to cause 'uneasiness in the parish'.

Local pubs tend to do well during Wimbledon tennis fortnight and it seems the Alexandra was perhaps the first to take advantage of this. In 1893, just sixteen years after the All England championships began, the Alexandra applied for an 'occasional licence for the purpose of providing refreshments during the All England Lawn Tennis Tournament'. It has to be remembered that at this time the club was not in Church Road as now, but in Worple Road, so the Alex was quite nearby.

Although by the twentieth century there were quite a number of pubs in Wimbledon it seems that the town centre ones were very wary of competitors and in 1934 the Alex and the South Western (opposite the station) were opposing the renewal of a drinks licence to Johnston's restaurant at the bottom of Wimbledon Hill. They were unsuccessful and three years later they, and also the Prince of Wales (at the top of Hartfield Road) this time, opposed the renewal of the same licence, again unsuccessfully.

But the Alex was to go on from strength to strength, increasing its size and winning an Evening Standard award in 1972. The plaque is still proudly displayed on the wall by the entrance to this day, though it is not clear what exactly the award was for. The wording says: 'Evening Standard Pub of the Year Contest, award winner 1972.' The winner of the Pub of the Year award that year though was the Victoria in Bermondsey, so perhaps the Alex was runner-up or won in another category.

But despite this official recognition the pub was under threat of closure just twelve years later. In 1984 Merton Council was planning to widen the road and had decided that the Alex would have to be demolished. The locals, luckily, had other ideas. Alex

The Alexandra (undated)

regular Jack Sheridean, a train driver, who had been using the pub since 1948 in his RAF days, started a campaign which gathered 7000 signatures and the pub was saved.

By 1998 the pub was doing well enough to expand and built the Smart Alex restaurant and wine bar next door in St Mark's place. Also by then there was a roof garden and recently a 'loft' bar has opened up alongside it. Today there are regular quiz nights and other events and it is a thriving pub right at the centre of Wimbledon.

The Alex also had its very own ghost though it has not been sighted recently. In 1991 a child was seen and heard calling for its mother by a member of staff in one of the upstairs rooms but it mysteriously disappeared when they turned away for a moment. When the pub was being redecorated a little while later a child's clothes were found in another room. Other staff reported strange experiences around this time in the staff quarters at the top of the pub. (For the full story see More Mysterious Wimbledon, published 1995.)

Amazingly, there was still a blacksmith's outside the pub in St Mark's Place until 1970.

A STATION PUB?

There could have been a pub at Wimbledon station if two local businessmen had had their way in 1891. An application was made to local magistrates for a licensed 'refreshment room' between the District line and the main line to Waterloo. The application was opposed not only by the local vicar, Canon Haygarth, and the licensees of all the nearby pubs, but also by the local board and the ratepayers' association. The applicants claimed that the local pubs were not the sort of places a father would want to take his wife or daughter to for refreshments and that they did not wish to compete with them anyway, but simply to provide a service to the more than a million passengers a year they claimed used the station. They also seemed to dismiss the vicar's objections on the grounds that the clergy were opposed to all drinks licences! The licence was refused.

WATERING DOWN THE WHISKEY

In 1922 the publicans of the Alexandra, the South Western Hotel and the Wimbledon Hill Hotel (Dog & Fox) were taken to the local police court for watering down their whiskey. Although the landlords offered various excuses they were fined between £10 and £20 each. Interestingly, the Alexandra had been accused of watering down its gin when a food inspector came in and ordered a pint (!) of it. On this occasion no prosecution had followed.

GARDEN SHED (FORMERLY HORSE & GROOM)

The Horse and Groom was in Haydon's Road by the 1830s. The first landlord was William Gibson, whose name appears in the 1838 rate book. At this time the immediate area was largely undeveloped with the houses in North, South and East Roads not to appear until 1852. Even as late as the 1860s much of the surrounding area was fields so the clientele would probably have been land workers, and later, the builders, carpenters, etc that would be constructing the new houses.

In 1859 the pub was granted a spirits licence. At this time many of the pubs were just simple beer houses so this elevated the Horse and Groom above many of its competitors. In fact, at the licensing meeting many other local pubs had applied for a spirits licence and David Upton, the owner of this pub, was the only person to be granted one.

A lease dated 1860 shows that the pub was a fairly substantial property with a north west room, a south east room, a middle room, parlour, bar, tap room, 'bar parlour', kitchen, etc. plus a cart shed and stable with three stalls, a shed with another two stalls, and a skittle ground with a pantile roof covering it. The rent at that time was £45 a year and the property was leased from the Union Brewery.

By the 1860s though the Horse & Groom had competition from other pubs and beer houses in the immediate vicinity. Just along Haydon's Road to the north was the British Queen and in the other direction not far away was the Marquis of Lorne. In the backstreets of North and South roads were many more small beer houses, all catering for the growing population of builders, railway workers and other artisans who were in the process of building Wimbledon as we now know it.

As with other local pubs of its time the Horse and Groom was used as a meeting place for local clubs and societies. In 1873 the Ancient Order of Foresters met here. They were not lumberjacks as may be suggested by the name but one of the early friendly societies that collected small subscriptions from its members and helped them out in time of need.

Twenty-three years after obtaining his spirits licence, landlord David Upton was fined in 1882 for watering down his rum. As it was his first offence the fine was just 12s 6d. Local magistrates were not so lenient in 1885 when a man named Walter Brookson was sent to prison for two months after being caught stealing two shillings from the pub's till.

It may have been thought that the concept of 'ladettes' or young women behaving badly after getting drunk was a recent phenomenon but in 1903 two 'violent young ladies' were arrested after creating a disturbance outside the Horse and Groom. They were given the option of either a ten shilling fine or seven days in jail.

The Horse and Groom was hit by a shell during World War Two on September 11, 1940 as were many other buildings in and around Haydon's Road and other parts of Wimbledon but it seems the damage was not too great and pub continued to function.

It is interesting that up until modern times the Horse and Groom remained an old-fashioned pub. An article in the Wimbledon News in 1998 tells how the new husband and wife team who had just taken over the pub went and introduced themselves to neighbours and when the pub reopened after a make-over they still designated Saturday night as 'dominoes night' and kept traditional games such as darts as well as concessions to the modern day with pool tables and juke boxes. In 2014 the pub name was changed to the Garden Shed (*see* Pub Names section).

Horse and Groom, 2003

Hill Rd., Wimbledon

Prince of Wales, c. 1910

PRINCE OF WALES

This pub has been at the top of Hartfield Road since 1867 when the landlord was William Amos Eagles. It seems to have started as a simple beer shop as in February 1867 Mr Eagles was in trouble with the police for having it open after 11.00 pm with twenty people drinking and smoking at the bar. When he was taken to court Mr Eagles said that he was seeking a licence for the house. He also said that some of his neighbours were in the habit of coming to the pub on a Tuesday evening to hear a song but said that no drinks were served after 11.00 pm. He was fined half a crown with two shillings costs.

The plot for a 'tavern' had been offered for sale as early as March 1863 but due to rebuilding of the station to accommodate the new Tooting and Merton lines building of the pub was delayed.

A few years ago there was a plaque outside claiming associations with highwaymen such as Dick Turpin but he was long dead and the highway robbery era long over when this pub was built. A Wimbledon News article in the 1990s claimed that it was a 17th century coaching inn but a glance at the 1865 Ordnance Survey map shows that there wasn't even a building on this spot at that time, let alone a coaching inn.

There is a strange entry in the JP's minutes of 1868 when William Eagles is granted a billiard licence but refused a victualler's licence! He continued to run it as a beer shop though and was still there in 1870.

In March 1868 a man was found injured on the nearby railway line and a doctor called to examine him. This was a year before Wimbledon's first hospital was opened so it was not unusual for a pub to be used in this way. The inquest, which was held at the Railway Tavern in Kingston, concluded that, under the influence of drink, he had fallen from a train coming from Waterloo and that no foul play had taken place.

As with other local pubs, the Prince of Wales was used for purposes other than drinking. In February 1869 an advert in the Sporting Life announced that a 'fine fat sheep' will be shot for by twelve members at half a crown each. It says there will be 'a good supply of birds.' A similar shooting match was advertised in December 1871 and was this time a pigeon shooting match for a 'fat ox'. Another one, in December 1873 advertised that the match would take place in a 'meadow adjoining the railway station.'

The pub later became quite a substantial enterprise. The census of 1881 shows that living there in addition to owner James Gould and his family were three barmaids, a housemaid, a waiter, and a billiard marker (a man who kept the score during games).

In 1884 local estate agent Alfred H.C. Olley held an auction here for 46 plots of land in Gap Road 'suitable for small villa residences or cottages'. Wimbledon was still being built at that stage. In 1886 Mr Olley was here again, selling houses in nearby Graham Road which were priced at £240 and £250 each. Even at 2021 prices this would only have been around £32,000 each.

Also that year there was a rather more macabre event when an inquest was held into the death of a man in Hartfield Road who had been found dead in bed with his throat cut. A verdict of suicide whilst in a state of temporary insanity was returned.

In May 1898 the pub was the venue for a meeting of the Royal Arthur Masonic lodge at which the pub laid on a meal and musical entertainment.

Anti-social behaviour is nothing new it seems. In 1894 the Wimbledon & District Gazette reported that a 'hammerman' from Merton Rush was charged with being drunk and disorderly after having been thrown out of the Prince of Wales Hotel and subsequently the South-Western public house. It was here that he was said to have 'run wildly about the road, interfering with foot passengers'. He was given the choice of a seven shillings and sixpence fine or seven days hard labour.

In the 1970s a lunchtime theatre was established here in an upstairs room. It was started by local actor Michael Robbins and his actress wife Hal Dyer. When The Wimbledon Pub Crawlers, as they were known – though despite their name they don't seem to have played at other pubs – began in 1974 Michael Robbins had already become well-known through his role as Arthur Rudge in TV sitcom On the Buses. The first season was planned to be just six plays but ended up as eighteen. The project had been first announced in The Stage as early as May 1973 but the first production was not staged until February 1974 when they put on How Now by Michael Sharp.

There were plays by well-known writers such as Johnny Speight and Tom Stoppard and also a young writer named Jonathan Lynn who was later to become better known as co-author of TV sitcom Yes Minister which began in 1980. Actress Patricia Hayes directed at least one play here. Plays were staged on Monday to Friday lunchtimes from 1.15 to 2.00 pm and on Wednesday evenings. Admission was 30p and a year's membership just 20p. Costumes were supplied by the Dancers & Fancy Dress shop in Hartfield Crescent. Other equipment was supplied by local businesses such as Gerry's in Wimbledon Broadway and Radio, TV and Entertainments also in the Broadway.

In 1974 the pub introduced the ancient game of Shuffleboard in the cellar bar and the Wimbledon News reported that takings had gone up by 10% as a result.

There had been some discussion nationally that year about the possibility of lowering the age at which people could buy alcoholic drinks in pubs. The manager here said he was in favour of it as it was difficult enough to differentiate between the sexes let alone the ages!

In 2007 there was a long-running saga in the Wimbledon Guardian about the pub's clock, which had not been working for some time. In July, Merton Council's leader, David Williams had urged the pub's owners, Punch Taverns, to have it repaired but they refused, saying the cost would run into many thousands of pounds. By August Wimbledon's MP Stephen Hammond had added his voice to the campaign to have the clock fixed. Later in August a clock repair company had offered to give a free quote for the repairs. The local Guardian continued to cover the story into September while the hands of the clock resolutely stayed at 12.00. In their September 6 issue they pointed out that the Chief Executive of Punch Taverns had earned over £11 million the previous year.

The clock was finally restored to working order by 2008. An article in the Wimbledon Society newsletter of September 2008 says that the clock was not there when the pub was first built but added when an extra storey was built in 1898. It seems though that there had been occasions in the past when the clock had stopped working and had been the subject of comment in the local papers, for example in 1923 and in 2000 when the clock had not been working for five years. According to the same article the clock was deemed by the Surrey Independent to be the 'recognised timekeeper of the town' when it was first put up in 1898.

There is also a separate venue in the basement of the pub: Bertie's Bar, which can be accessed either through the pub or via the courtyard in Hartfield Road. This bar opened in 1971. The Wimbledon News claimed in 1998 that Tommy Steele had been here – presumably when appearing at Wimbledon Theatre – and passed on a rumour that he may have even written 'Crash Bang Wallop What a Picture' (sic) here. He did indeed appear in Half A Sixpence at Wimbledon Theatre in 1963 in a pre-West End run of the show before its transfer to the Cambridge Theatre, and one of the songs was Flash Bang Wallop, but it was not written by Tommy Steele. In fact, Wimbledon Theatre believes the song may have been written in their 'piano bar' by the show's composer and lyricist David Heneker.

Today the pub is part of the Greene King chain and remains a popular pub at the heart of Wimbledon.

Note: In March 1871 Joseph John Harrison applied for beer and spirit licences for 'The Railway Hotel' Hartfield Road. At first glance this might have been taken as an alternative name for the Prince of Wales, but in the same licensing session William Amos Eagles successfully applied for beer and spirit licences for the Prince of Wales Hotel. There seems to be no other reference in the records to the Railway Hotel so it remains a mystery as to where exactly it was or was proposed to be.

A PUB FOR OLIVER CROMWELL?

At the local magistrates' licensing session in March 1891 Mr Oliver Cromwell, a builder from Chislehurst, applied for a licence for a pub he intended to build at the corner of Gap Road and Haydon's Road. It was to be called The Station Hotel. He claimed that the public should have an opportunity to get a glass of beer without having to travel a quarter of a mile. He was supported by Mr Ackermann, an overseer and also owner of the South Western Hotel, but the licence was opposed by the local temperance group who pointed out that most of the new houses built nearby were unoccupied. The licence was refused.

RAYNES PARK TAVERN/HOTEL

It had been thought that this pub was not here before about 1873 but a recently-discovered newspaper report from July 15, 1871 announces a sale of building land at the Raynes Park Tavern. This was three months before the station opened. The land was on the Cottenham Park estate. Surprisingly, one of the prime plots of land was given away as a prize at the National Rifle Association meeting that week. It sounds though that the Raynes Park Tavern may not yet have been fully functioning as a pub as in April 1872 Mr Gresham Aikman, who had sold the land the previous year, was auctioning off the remaining plots at the Swan in the Ridgway, and was also selling the Raynes Park Tavern. It is described as being 'fitted, regardless of cost, with every convenience for carrying on the business of a licensed victualler.'

In March 1874 the landlord, Mr Tebbut, arranged a sparrow shooting match in the grounds at the back of the pub. Thirteen men competed for a first prize of a plated cup and a second prize of a silver watch and chain. Each competitor was given five birds to shoot at. In the newspaper announcement of this event the pub is called the Raynes Park Hotel whereas previously it had always been referred to as the Raynes Park Tavern. The name wasn't changed back to the Raynes Park Tavern until 1990.

By 1875 it was being run by William Eagles who had run the Prince of Wales in Wimbledon from 1867 to 1874. He put an announcement in the Surrey Comet in August 1875 saying that he had just bought the pub and made various improvements, including the addition of a billiard room with two 'first class' tables.

As with other local pubs of this era, The Raynes Park Tavern was used to hold inquests and in 1878 a strange verdict was recorded regarding the death of a 74-year-old man who was said to have died from syncope, 'no doubt on having eaten too hearty a supper'.

It is worth remembering that in 1878 Raynes Park was still a semi-rural area. An announcement in the Surrey Advertiser that year gives details of an auction at this pub for lots of 15–20 acres of 'luxuriant crops of grass now growing on about 120 acres of meadow land, being part of Raynes Park Farm'.

In 1881 the pub was burgled by 'three lads' who were caught at Wimbledon station with several items taken from the pub and sentenced to twelve months hard labour.

By 1881 the landlord of the pub was Thomas Savage, and perhaps living up to his name, was accused in April 1883 of encouraging fighting on the premises. Police had been called to a disturbance at the pub with several men fighting and the police constable said the landlord had not only failed to stop the fighting but could not walk straight himself! Mr Savage was fined ten shillings but kept his licence as he had previously run an orderly pub.

Thomas Savage was still running the pub in 1889 when a fox terrier coursing meeting was held in Raynes Park and owners wishing to enter had to apply at the pub. It is not shown where exactly the meeting was held but at this stage in the area's development there was still a lot of open land.

RAYNES PARK, WIMBLEDON.

T 112

Raynes Park Tavern/Hotel, c. 1910

In 1901 Thomas Savage was reported in the papers to have taken on a wager to walk a quarter of a mile, ride on horseback for a quarter of a mile, swim in the river for a quarter of a mile, run a quarter of a mile, cycle a quarter of a mile and then row a quarter of a mile. It was reported that he completed the six-part event on the Kingston towpath in just eighteen and a half minutes. At the time, the landlord would have been 56 or 57 years old, so it possible that the feat was completed by his son, also Thomas John Savage, who would have been 21 or 22.

Mr Savage obviously liked his sport as a couple of years later he organised a 'laundresses' sealed handicap walk' which started and finished at the pub.

Mr Savage had a son named Henry who had lived at the pub from the age of three and who became a writer and a friend of D.H. Lawrence. He served in the army in the Boer War, wrote a biography of the poet Richard Middleton and an autobiography entitled The Receding Shore. D.H. Lawrence wrote several letters to Savage in 1913 in which he implores him not to feel he has to impress his friends and neighbours in Raynes Park. It seemed that Savage was working on a book entitled Barber's Bun and wished to show the people in Raynes Park that he could get it published. Lawrence said 'Why don't you hate Raynes Park and tell it to go to hell?' D.H. Lawrence had become a friend after Savage gave a favourable review to Lawrence's first novel, The White Peacock. Savage edited magazines as well as writing volumes of poetry, a novel, and other books.

An article in the Liverpool Echo in December 1933 talks of his 'studies of Bohemian life during the last ten years.' Savage was also quoted as saying that D.H. Lawrence had confided to him that he himself would like to be a pub owner! From this article we also learn that Savage's father Thomas, had taken over the pub after returning from 'railway work in India'.

In June 2004 the pub's owners put out an appeal for information about the history of the pub and were told that it had been extended in 1904, hence that date being shown just above the entrance.

One regular remembered the pub in the Second World War being a 'clutter of steel helmets, gas masks, and rifles as civilians and service personnel crowded in between the air raids. The feeling seemed to be that if your number was up you might as well be enjoying yourself rather than huddling in an air raid shelter.

The pub was refurbished in 1972 with 'Edwardian-look' chandeliers, gold cornices, pillars, balustrades and flock wallpaper. There was also a bream in a glass case, and another glass case containing a stuffed fox carrying a duck. Not all the regulars were impressed. One commented to the local paper that he 'wouldn't dream of going in the lounge bar now – it looks like a ruddy brothel.' He said he'd stick to the public bar which still had darts and simple red lino on the floor.

In 2004 the pub became a temporary public library until 2005 when the newly built Raynes Park library opened in Kingston Road.

Today, the pub seems to be flourishing and is still something of a landmark right at the centre of Raynes Park.

SULTAN

This pub has been in Norman Road since at least 1868 when it was being run by Walter Goldsmith. As with other local pubs, it was used as an estate agents when sellers of land or property would have details available to look at here. In the 1880s the area was still being developed and plots of land nearby were being sold off for housebuilding.

In the 1890s it was also used as a football changing room. From 1892–95 there are several reports in the local papers of Wimbledon FC changing here before matches played at the recreation ground on the corner of Quicks Road and Haydon's Road. The team that was to lift the FA cup in 1988 had begun as The Old Centrals in 1889 when playing on Wimbledon Common and used first the Fox and Grapes and later the Swan as their changing rooms. Teams that played here include: Clapham, Balham Wanderers, Pickwick, Kingston-on-Thames and East Sheen. The newspaper announcements would include the quaint instruction 'dress at The Sultan'.

In 1898 the landlord, Thomas Porter, was taken to court by a woman who had been thrown out of the pub. Surprisingly, the case took up almost two whole days of court time with the woman claiming to have been assaulted by the landlord and called a 'beastly woman'. The landlord denied using force and the magistrates decreed that the landlord had the right to eject any person who was drunken, violent, quarrelsome or disorderly and that he had been acting within his rights.

Unfortunately the pub was bombed in 1944 and had to be rebuilt. It had been owned by Thorne Brothers brewery up until the 1920s and later by Friary Meux, Ind Coope and then Taylor Walker who sold it in 1994 to the Hopback Brewery. It is the Salisbury-based brewery's only London pub. The bomb which badly damaged the pub hit on February 4, 1944 and that, and another four bombs, destroyed twenty-seven houses, seriously damaged a further forty-eight and caused minor damage to another three hundred and twenty. The rebuilding of the pub was carried out by Friary Meux.

The pub had a colourful landlord in the 1950s, George 'Jack' Wife, who was an ex-boxer, 'chucker out' in American saloons and who had gone into business at the age of ten selling cat's meat in the street and later ran away to sea 'in case things got dull'. In September 1958 he left Wimbledon to run a pub in Peterborough.

The pub was CAMRA's South West London Pub of the Year in 2018 – an award which it had won several times previously. It was also Time Out magazine's London pub of the year in 2004.

Today it holds regular quiz nights and music nights and has an annual beer festival in September. It is a small, friendly local and retains the atmosphere of a traditional community pub.

PUB OF THE YEAR

Between 2009 and 2018 the CAMRA SW London Pub of the Year award was given to an SW19 pub seven times out of the ten. Four times for the Trafalgar in High Path, twice for the Sultan and once for the Hand in Hand on Wimbledon Common.

Sultan, 2003

Woodman, c. 1910

WOODMAN

The Woodman was in Durnsford Road by 1860 but not at the present site. It was further south, just by the railway bridge and in fact the original building is still there at 204 Durnsford Road and is used as offices.

In 1860 the Woodman Tavern as it was then known was being run by Mary Carpenter and at that time the surrounding area was largely undeveloped. To the north was Wimbledon Park Farm and a large house named Woodside and to the west were Vineyardhill Woods and the lake that is now part of Wimbledon Park. Nearby was the woodman's cottage – presumably occupied by the man who looked after surrounding woodland. As there were so few houses nearby it is likely that the pub was catering mainly for the various people working on the land.

It was up for sale in 1892 with a 23-year lease and had a house adjoining called Elm Lodge. By May 1901 the 'former Woodman Tavern' was for sale. It is advertised as having twelve rooms, stabling, and a large garden. It is believed that the pub moved in 1898 to its present position which is where the house named Woodside once stood.

The pub was modernised in 1973 and what were previously four separate bars became one public bar, and one large saloon bar. Thatch was put over the bar and woodcutters' tools placed on display. One regular, who had been going there since 1935, said that they had ruined it.

An article in the Wimbledon News in 1998 claimed that the pub has played host to many celebrities over the years from actor Oliver Reed to members of Wimbledon Football Club as well as tennis stars such as Arantxa Sanchez-Vicario who apparently visited the pub with her family several times in 1997. It also says that many actors appearing at Wimbledon theatre used the pub.

They forgot to mention another VIP customer, future Prime Minister Theresa May. She was a councillor for the Wimbledon Park ward (then Durnsford ward) from 1986–94 and a 2017 article in the Wimbledon Guardian shows a picture of her in the Woodman in 2012.

The Woodman was sold by Greene King in 2017 to property company Goldcrest and there were concerns that it might be closed down but happily, it reopened in 2019 and some of the land was used for new housing.

THE GOOD OLD DAYS

In 1974 the Merton and Morden News ran a series of features entitled Looking in at Your Local, where a reporter visited a pub each week and gave comments on decor, clientele, food, etc. And what a different world it was. Some pubs were just converting from traditionally separate public, private, saloon and lounge bars to bigger, open plan areas, and many still had quite old-fashioned entertainment with pianists and singalongs. Food seems incredibly cheap by today's standards with a ham sandwich at 15p or a shepherd's pie for 25p. This was a decade after the Swinging 60s but it seems that some traditions clung on for much longer. It is a long way from today's gastro pubs, Thai cuisine and £5 pints! A pint of light and bitter in one of the pubs then was just 18p and a gin & tonic 26p.

PAST PUBS (18TH AND 19TH CENTURY ORIGIN)

'When you have lost your inns drown your empty selves,
for you will have lost the last of England'
Hilaire Belloc (This and That and The Other, 1912)

It is said that when Belloc was writing his book The Stane Street (published in 1913) he sometimes drank in the Prince of Wales on Morden Road which was near the line of the old Roman road. That pub is still there, but Belloc might have been shocked and saddened to see how many others nearby have closed down since he wrote the above warning. The following are all pubs that were there when Belloc was alive but have since gone – many in just the last few years.

BAY TREE

A strange one this, as sometimes it is listed in local directories and other sources as a 'temperance coffee house' but in others the owner is shown as a 'licensed victualler'. It was in Kingston Road on the corner of Montague Road from 1878 when it was being run by Robert Love who was described in the 1881 census as a licensed victualler. An 1884 newspaper refers to it as the Bay Tree Coffee Palace when there is a meeting of the Wimbledon and Merton Radical Association here. The following year, the same group are reported to be meeting at the Bay Tree Inn! In 1889 a meeting is announced, to be chaired by John Innes, on the formation of the Manor Club, but this time it is called the Bay Tree Assembly Room. By 1891 it is listed in the directory as Bay Tree Coffee Tavern and Bay Tree Assembly Rooms. It was by then part of a row called Campbell Terrace. At one point the Bay Tree was owned by John Innes and arrangements were made for the children of poor fathers to eat there free of charge. In the Wimbledon News of April 1900 there is an advert for The Bay Tree Temperance Hotel. It offered a' large room for cyclists, football and all athletic clubs' and a 'small room for smaller parties', as well as a large garden. By 1914 the address shows The Bay Tree Adult School. The building was rebuilt in 2000 and became an estate agents.

BRITANNIA

There is just a single mention of this pub in Plough Lane in an 1867 directory. It was being run by Charles Henry Brown who is described as a beer retailer. It is likely then that this was simply a small, short-lived beer shop.

BEER SHOPS

In 1830 an act of Parliament was passed which deregulated the pub trade. Rather than having to apply for a full licence, anyone could pay two guineas and open a beer shop. The owners were not permitted to sell spirits and the idea was to discourage people from drinking them. Many people ran beer shops as sidelines to their usual profession, which would have been in trades such as plumbing, carpentry or bricklaying. Many of these enterprises were short-lived though some continued for many decades and eventually became fully-licensed pubs. In a working class area such as North and South Roads, off Haydon's Road, there were quite large numbers of these beer shops, almost too many for the small area in which they were competing not only with one another but also with fully-licensed pubs nearby.

British Queen

BRITISH QUEEN

This pub was at the corner of North Road and Haydon's Road by 1860 when it was being run by Charles Brookes and was thus the second pub in this road after the Horse & Groom and before the Marquis of Lorne.

In the Wimbledon & District Gazette of March 6, 1897 we find the then licensee Mr G. Mildenhall being charged in court with allowing a man to be 'made drunk in his house', which was described as a serious offence. A Mr Bell of the Licensed Victuallers Association appeared on his behalf and stated that Mr Mildenhall had been running the pub for thirty years without a complaint having been made against him. The 'thirty years' is not borne out by the records though, which show a different landlord there before 1891. As the case was unproven Mr Mildenhall was allowed to keep his licence as were 89 other people in the area who had theirs renewed!

At the same court session, a grocer (Mr Greenwood at 155 Haydon's Road), successfully applied for a licence to sell bottled beer even though he was only five doors away from this pub. The magistrate said he thought it 'better for a man to have an opportunity of buying beer at a shop of this kind than to be obliged to go to a public house where he may be tempted to drink spirits and stop considerably longer than he ought.' The local temperance society was still in operation at this time and perhaps magistrates were bearing this in mind. Indeed, a Mr Hiley, who ran an off-licence in Dundonald Road, had a licence refused at this session for beer and wine to be drunk on the premises. A Mr Geake, of the temperance society, said that as the shop was opposite a school it was 'undesirable that the children should be constantly witnessing an exhibition of the effects of drink.'

The Surrey Comet of October 14, 1905 reported an attempted suicide at the pub. The billiard marker shared a bedroom with 35-year-old barman James Frost and when he went upstairs at 11.00 pm found Frost hanging from the bedpost with a scarf around his neck. A police constable cut the man down and he was taken to hospital. A week later Frost was taken to Wimbledon police court and charged with attempted suicide. He was bound over for six months.

The pub was sold in 1911 with a 69-year lease for £5,200 (about £617,000 in 2021)

As late as the 1920s The British Queen sounded like a friendly old-fashioned community pub. Violette Wright, who lived in the area in the 1920s as a child, remembered that the pub still had a bar with sawdust on the floor and that customers could buy bread from a home-baked cottage loaf with matured cheese. Her grandfather also said the ale was good! She remembers that she and the other children were put in a barrow outside the pub and given either a large Brighton Biscuit 'the size of a saucer', or an Arrowroot one. Her grandfather also gave the landlord onions and runner beans from his allotment when in season.

The pub was rebuilt in 1901 and in the 1990s changed its name to 'Haydon's', finally closing down in 1999 and being given over to residential use.

Freeman Arms, later The Broadway

BROADWAY (FORMERLY FREEMAN ARMS)

This pub was originally called the Freeman Arms and was here by 1865 when being run by David Paxton, who five years previously had been running the livery and bait stables at the Rose & Crown in Wimbledon Village. He then ran the Dog & Fox for a while, around 1862, as in October 1863 the licence for it is being transferred from him to one John Collins.

He had previously had a couple of brushes with the law. Once in January 1848 when he and his brother and another man were before local magistrates for trespassing in search of game on Warren Farm, Wimbledon Common. Nothing was proved and they went free. In 1861 Paxton was in court being accused of injuring a horse left in his care at the livery stables during the NRA meeting on the common. It was decided that any injury had been accidental and again, he was not charged.

One of the first things he did when taking over the Freeman Arms was to apply for a billiards licence. He may have even been here before 1865 as on January 14 of that year he is advertising dogs for sale from the pub and on January 28 organising a sparrow shoot there. In February another bird shoot was planned with a 'fine home-fed fat pig' as the prize. Also, in March 1864 Paxton had withdrawn an application for a licence for 'a house in New Wimbledon'.

By May the following year the pub had been taken over by Edward George Kennard, who continued with the sparrow shooting matches, organising one in July of that year with this time, six home-cured hams as prizes. The shooting continued through the year, then in October the pub was taken over by John Paxton, presumably a relative of the first owner. The pub changed hands again in January 1871 and the new owner was Joshua Rose. The shooting matches seem to have stopped by then and the pub was being used as a venue for the sale or auction of land locally. In March, freehold building land with 'frontage to the new roads called Russell, Gladstone and Herbert Roads' was being sold. The development of 'New Wimbledon' continued apace. Before he had left, John Paxton had complained to the Home Secretary about street lighting and as a consequence of that the road (presumably the Broadway) was 'adopted' by the local board and five gas lamps erected. Mr Paxton also provided a public convenience at the pub. Joshua Rose didn't remain landlord for long. In July 1872 the new owner was Charles Fletcher.

As with other pubs of this era, the Freeman Arms was a meeting place for various clubs and societies. In March 1872 the annual meeting of the Merton Club was held here with president Henry Peek MP presiding. In December 1881 the local fire brigade held their annual dinner here. At that time the firemen were all volunteers and the fire station was in Wimbledon Village. The evening ended in a sing song with two fireman providing musical accompaniment on guitar and 'organette'. In March 1894 it was the venue for the first annual dinner of the Wimbledon Swimming Club. The Wimbledon and Merton Swimming baths had opened in Worple Road the previous year and preceded those in Latimer Road by eight years.

Also that same year an off-licence at the corner of Latimer Road applied for a licence to sell draught beer on the premises, effectively turning it into a beer shop/pub that would be in direct competition with the Freeman Arms. The landlord of the pub, and also the landlord of The Grove at South Wimbledon successfully opposed the licence, as did the Church of England Temperance Society. It must be remembered that even at this late stage Wimbledon Broadway and surrounding roads were still being developed – the photo on the back cover of this book shows cows grazing in the fields that were later to be developed as the bottom part of Wimbledon Broadway. It was natural therefore that as the area developed and the population increased so did the competition to sell beer to the people in the area.

In 1882 the landlord of the pub, William Palmer had been summonsed for selling 'adulterated spirits'. An inspector had ordered a pint of gin and a pint of rum, which upon analysis proved to be watered down. The landlord was fined 20 shillings, with 25 shillings costs.

The pub was also, like others nearby, the venue for inquests. One, conducted here in August 1890 was by Athelstan Braxton Hicks, son of John Braxton Hicks, the famous obstetrician. Mr Braxton Hicks was sometimes known as 'the children's coroner' due to his special interest in conducting enquiries into baby farming and the unexplained deaths of children. The case heard at the Freeman Arms however was straightforward enough, though tragic. A 7-year-old boy had run into the road to retrieve a marble when he was run over by a horse-drawn bread van. The driver had not seen the boy and only realised something was amiss when he heard the screams of his mother. He was exonerated from any blame. Mr Braxton Hicks was the coroner for South West London from 1885 onwards and conducted many inquests locally.

The freehold of the pub and adjoining land was up for sale in 1907. Then, according to information from Courage Brewery, the pub was bought by Hodgson's Brewery (later part of Courage) in 1912 from London United Tramways. An insurance document dated 1936 shows the pub being referred to as The Broadway Hotel and The Freeman Arms, so it could be that it was seen as two separate enterprises: The Freeman Arms pub, and the Broadway Hotel.

In the 1970s the Broadway continued as a traditional pub with a dartboard and music evenings featuring a woman playing an electric organ.

By 1974 the pub was being run by a family of musicians. Bill Prior, his mother and two sisters had performed in pubs and clubs as the 'Prio Trio' with a line-up of accordion, piano and drums. A Texan customer (presumably from nearby American firm Brown & Root) was impressed at the family atmosphere, commenting that back home a woman couldn't walk into a bar without being propositioned. To add to the pub's homely atmosphere the most popular lunchtime sandwich was one of bread and dripping at a princely 2.5p!

The pub carried on as the Broadway Hotel or the Broadway Tavern until the 1990s when it began to undergo a number of identity changes. First it was known as Jim Thompson's Flaming Wok, then The Dragon and Broadway, then The House Bar, and then The Prophecy, a private members' club, until becoming a branch of Italian-themed restaurant chain Made in Italy.

THE BROADWAY PUB THAT NEVER WAS

In March 1887 an application was put in for a licence for an establishment known as the Iddesleigh Hotel at the corner of Merton Road and Latimer Road. It was argued that the recreation ground in Quicks Road had no changing rooms and that this establishment could also be used for that purpose. In the 1890s the Old Centrals/Wimbledon FC team used the Sultan as their changing room (see entry for Sultan). The application was refused after being opposed by all the other nearby pubs, including the Freeman Arms. An application for a hotel with that name at that location was put in again in March 1894 but again refused.

Another Pub That Never Was

This sign (now sadly painted over) at the corner of Palmerston Road and Kingston Road certainly looks like a pub sign depicting Lord Palmerston, but there was never a pub here. There was however an off licence for over a hundred years, from the early twentieth century until quite recently.

DUKE OF CAMBRIDGE

This pub was in North Road, just off Haydon's Road by 1881 when it was being run by Thomas Hatcher. By this time there were not just the three pubs in Haydon's Road but several others in North and South Roads, though they would have been simple beer shops as this one was. Though in some directories the pub was shown at numbers 39 and 41 North Road so may have been more substantial than some of the other back street beer shops nearby. It had several changes of owner before closing in 1926.

OFF LICENCES

These days it is rare to see an off licence, but in the Victorian era there were more of them in Wimbledon than there were pubs. A list from the petty sessions of 1890 shows more than forty of them. They were in Wimbledon Broadway and many of the roads off the Broadway as well as in and around Haydon's Road, Kingston Road and Merton High Street. There were three in Hartfield Road alone and two in Hartfield Crescent plus several more on Wimbledon Hill and in the Village. Off licences had come into being following William Gladstone's 1860 Refreshment Houses Act which he introduced when Chancellor of the Exchequer so perhaps it is appropriate there was also one in Gladstone Road! And perhaps it is no surprise that the temperance campaigners were attempting to curtail drinking in the face of so many places where alcohol could be purchased.

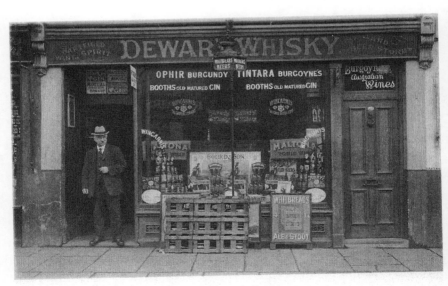

Off licence in Hartfield Road

Duke of Edinburgh

DUKE OF EDINBURGH

This pub was in Kingston Road at the corner of Southey Road by 1869 when it was being run by Robert Lemon whose first licence had been granted in March of that year. The area bounded by Kingston Road, Hartfield Road, Merton Road and Wimbledon Broadway had only been developed in the 1850s, having been mainly farmland up till then. A map of 1853 shows the new roads to be laid out: Griffith, Pelham, Southey and Montague; and the area at the corner of Southey and Kingston Roads was earmarked for a 'tavern'. The Church of England had put the land up for sale in 1854, and the plots reserved for a tavern had been purchased by John Williams of Long Acre, Middlesex. It was to be ten years though before he sold the land on to a Merton builder by the name of Thomas Batchelor in 1864. Four years later in turn sold it on to Robert Lemon, and by now there was a building on the plot intended to be the new pub. Lemon paid £1,075.00. In June 1869 Batchelor leased to Lemon a house known as 3 Kingston Terrace and land adjoining the rear of the pub with an option to buy the freehold in seven years. Over the next few years there was much wheeling and dealing with this land and property as well as others nearby. By 1882 the freehold of the pub was purchased by George Gabb who had appeared in the previous year's directory as the licensee. It cost him £3,000.00. He in turn sold it to the brewers Charringtons in 1894. By 1919 Charringtons had granted a thirty-year lease to what would be the pub's final owner, Henry John Risdon.

It seems that from the outset Robert Lemon had big ambitions for this pub. In July 1870 he had put an advert in the Morning Advertiser reading: 'The place to spend a pleasant day. The Duke of Edinburgh Hotel and tavern, assembly rooms and pleasure grounds, New Wimbledon, Surrey. Two minutes from the site of the double gates, four minutes from the Wimbledon and Lower Merton stations.' (John Innes would later persuade the railway authorities to rename the station Merton Park to make it sound more upmarket for his new garden suburb of that name). The advert went on: 'Rooms suitable for Masonic banquets, assemblies, clubs, sales by auction, public meetings and bean feasts. Cricket, croquet, bowls, quoits, gymnasium etc., etc.' Note, there was no tennis as the All England championships were not to begin until 1877 so the game was not perhaps widely played at this point.

By September The Sportsman was reporting on a quoits match held here between two 'celebrated players'. By the following January Mr Lemon was advertising his 'music hall' at the pub every Monday and Saturday. He also mentioned the bowling green, cricket pitch and football field and gymnasium as well as livery and bait stables and private rooms for parties. Also, in a February advert he said he had engaged some first-rate talent 'regardless of expense'. It included 'Miss Bella Seagrave, the A1 characteristic serio-comic', and 'Mr William Bishop, star comic vocalist from the Provinces'. There was also a 'pantomimist' and 'Comic Irish duettists'. The landlord was also advertising a 'select Quadrille party' every Wednesday. By April he had also added a skittle ground to the list of attractions the pub had to offer as well as a printed tariff of dinners that could be sent to interested parties.

Sadly, this impressive start was not to continue as in June 1871 an advert appeared in the Morning Advertiser saying that the pub was to be auctioned off 'in consequence of recent domestic afflictions'. There had been an announcement in the Morning Advertiser on March 21 that Robert Lemon's only son, also Robert, had died, aged

29. No cause of death was given. It looks as though Mr Lemon had gamely tried to continue running the pub as the week before the auction announcement he had been advertising it and its many attractions which now included athletic sports and American bowls. With the pub came a 'ball and concert room' and stabling as well as the previously advertised amenities. The advert also mentions that the National Rifle Association meetings are held nearby (on the common) and also the 'rapid growth of the neighbourhood'. And it certainly was rapid. In 1861 the population of Wimbledon had been 4644 and by 1871 it had almost doubled to 9087. Ten years later it would be 15,950, and by 1891 25,761.

In May 1871 the Duke of Edinburgh had been advertised as 'The best way to the races' – presumably Epsom. Derby Day was in those days a huge social event with stalls and entertainments all along the route from London.

Despite the pub's wide appeal, it was still unsold by December 1871. Indeed, in September Mr Lemon had been advertising for a new pot man/ostler to work there.

The next we hear of the pub is in November 1872 when the pot man was in court charged with stealing nine bottles of wine which he had hidden in the pub's pigsty. The new landlord, Richard Henry Tear, had sacked the pot man after checking the cellar and finding the wine missing.

As if the pub was not busy enough with all its activities we find it being used in 1874 for military training. F Battery had company and carbine drill here at 8.00 pm on August 8. Then in 1879 it was the venue for the gathering of the Scottish Societies of London. The event was held on the August bank holiday and consisted of many sporting events such as tossing the caber, throwing the hammer, wrestling, tug of war and dancing the Highland Fling etc. The event concluded with dinner and singing, finishing with Auld Lang Syne.

According to the 1881 census the pub employed a 'billiard marker' which was a man who kept the scores at the billiard table and also kept the drinks topped up!

The billiard marker had made a gruesome discovery a couple of years previously when he found the dead body of the pub's pot man in a cupboard. It was reported in the Surrey Advertiser of January 12, 1878 that the 37-year-old pot man had been 'subject to fits'.

Through the 1880s and 90s and into the twentieth century the pub's grounds were widely used for sporting events, both public, and for businesses such as The Daily Graphic newspaper and Messrs E. and H. Hora, a local carriage company.

There was a tragedy here in 1895 when one of the barmen was found dead with his throat cut and a razor by his side. It was deemed to be suicide as the man had previously attempted to end his life by jumping into the Thames from Putney Bridge. Two years later, the landlord's 17-year-old daughter, who had been working there as a barmaid, committed suicide by laying down in front of a train at Tooting after her parents barred her from seeing a boyfriend who lived nearby.

The popularity of the pub as a venue for organised events continued well into the twentieth century. As late as 1933 the Wimbledon and District Rabbit Society was holding its annual show here. The pub had been the meeting place for various clubs and societies over the years including the Freemasons' Royal Arthur Lodge who had met here since their formation in 1871 until 1875 when they moved to the lecture hall in Lingfield Road. Also meeting here were the Southey Bowling Club, the Piscatorial Club and no less than sixteen different cycling clubs. It was said to be a 'nice run down to the country' from here for cyclists. Indeed, at the time this pub was built it was virtually on the edge of London with the countryside not far away.

Unfortunately the pub was bombed in the Second World War and closed in 1954. A reporter from the Wimbledon Borough News called into what was left of the pub in January 1954 and described the ruined building: 'The floor has mostly caved in to reveal great earthenware port wine vats heaped in confusion in the cellar. Half the bar remained in mid-air as it were, the verdigrised pumps still defiantly at attention. On the wall hung the mouldering remains of a dartboard.'

It seems that despite this scene of devastation the pub was still operating as the reporter talked to regulars and a couple of the recent landlords. The last of the landlords, Mr Risdon, had apparently laid out a £1,500 Cumberland bowling green at the back of the pub.

On the site of the pub today is Wimbledon fire station.

JOINERS ARMS

The pub was in South Road, just off Haydon's Road by 1868 when run by William Voller, but the name, Joiners Arms, wasn't shown in local directories until 1881. In the census of that year we find that the owner, still William Voller, is listed as a carpenter and beer retailer, hence the pub's name. His son, Robert, aged 15, is shown as a carpenter and an 'assistant in the business' so it sounds as though the beer shop was something of a sideline. The pub continued under other owners until 1914 – the cessation of the business perhaps being caused by the outbreak of World War One.

South Road, along with North Road and East Road had been laid out in the early 1850s so as more people, mainly workmen and their families, moved in so the beer houses began to appear.

JUNCTION TAVERN

This pub, at the Raynes Park end of Kingston Road was here by 1865 when being run by George Chittenden. An application for a licence for the Junction Tavern had been submitted by David Rickman White in March 1864 but does not seem to have been approved. Despite its name it was here before Raynes Park station opened (1871) and indeed was one of the first buildings in the area. Evelyn Jowett, who wrote a history of Raynes Park, believes that there may even have been some sort of temporary pub, possibly a mobile structure that served the men working on the railway. Again, we seem to have an area built on beer!

An advert in the London City Press of April 1868 shows the pub for sale and notes that it has stabling. Perhaps there was a reasonable amount of land attached to the pub as in 1885 we find someone being taken to court for stealing a goose from here. He was given the option of either a ten shilling fine or seven days in jail.

Around this time the pub was also used as a football changing room. There was a field opposite where matches were played. Not all teams were local. In 1888 we find the Westminster Association Senior Cup match being played here. Wimbledon FC played here in 1901 against a team named Emeriti.

In 1892 there had been a tragedy here. Two labourers had had an argument in the pub and decided to settle it with a fight in the field opposite. After a few minutes John Lovesay decided to walk away and shook hands with his opponent, William Morgan, but as he was putting his coat on Morgan, whose nickname was 'Boxer' due to his fighting skills, hit him again and the fight restarted with Lovesay delivering a fatal blow to Morgan's head. At the inquest, conducted by Mr Braxton Hicks at Kingston Union workhouse it was said that the men had been sober when fighting but it was later stated that they had been drinking in the Junction Tavern for seven hours before the fight began at 7.00 pm. Mr Braxton Hicks expressed his doubt that they could have been sober after drinking for so long. The case went to the Old Bailey and the jury decided that because Lovesay had been reluctant to fight he was only guilty of manslaughter and he was released.

In 1906 there was another tragedy when the landlord of the pub, Walter Chandler, shot himself dead with a shotgun. The inquest heard that he had suffered from ill-health and depression. It was believed that he used a gun-cleaning stick to fire the weapon.

Even in 1910 the area around the pub was still semi-rural and it was chosen to be the new 'country quarters' of Tooting Athletic Club. From here they would have eight-mile cross-country runs. Also that year it was the start and finish point for a ten-mile walking race with competitors from as far afield as North London and Kent. The pub provided a tea at the end of the day.

Evelyn Jowett said that in 1914 although there had been some development in Raynes Park it was patchy and that it was 'more countryside than suburb'. Farming still continued as well, with nearby Moat Farm surviving until the 1920s.

In the 1970s the pub was popular with bus drivers and conductors – presumably when they were off duty! It was still quite a thriving place then but over the next couple of decades seemed to lose popularity. In 2012 it was converted into a restaurant and a couple of years after that became a pub again, The Railhouse. It did not seem to be functioning for long before it closed again. In 2021 there were rumours that it is to be converted to retail use and flats.

Note: just along the road eastwards is a boundary stone on the wall of the next building showing the division between the parishes of Wimbledon and Merton. It appears to be dated 1866. Perhaps the Junction Tavern would have been a good refreshment stop for those beating the bounds in this area at that time.

KING'S HEAD

Was this the oldest pub in Wimbledon? Before it was rebuilt in 1934 it proudly proclaimed on its front wall that it dated back to 1496. Even the rebuilt pub showed that date above the entrance to the public bar. No proof of this date has ever been found but we know from the victuallers list it was there from at least 1725 when it was being run by one Peter Fry. Tantalisingly, Mr Fry is listed as the landlord of the 'Old King's Head' while a Peter Campion is shown as running the 'New King's Head'.

However, a victuallers' list of 1721 does not show the pub/s at all. Also, in 1637 the so-called 'water poet' John Taylor carried out a survey of inns around the country and mentioned others nearby, but not this one. There is one theory though that because the site of the inn is opposite what was once Merton Priory that it could have served as an outlet for excess ale that the monks produced for themselves. The priory was there until the Dissolution in 1538. It seems then that the pub may have existed before the early 18th century but so far no concrete evidence has been found.

In 1801 the landlord of the pub, Mr Woodman, was robbed by a highwayman at Balham. He gave him a few shillings, but soon afterwards, an ostler from another inn joined him in pursuing the highwayman, apprehending him and having him arrested. On August 6 the highwayman, John Norlidge, alias John Harris, was sentenced to death. On the same day others received the death sentence for lesser offences such as stealing a lamb or the carcass of a sheep.

We know that around this time the landlord of the pub was running a carriage service as on March 24, 1803 he advertised the business for sale in the Morning Post. He advertised a 'very desirable, profitable business in the glass coach and posting line.' The stock comprised: 'a glass coach, ten post horses, a chariot, and two post chaises, a gig, etc., etc.'. Whoever bought it would presumably have continued the business at the inn as Merton High Street was a main coaching route and it was also part of the posting route.

At the end of 1803 an interesting meeting was held here. All the mill owners and manufacturers along the Wandle gathered to discuss putting forward to Parliament an objection to a proposal for a canal running from Croydon to Portsmouth. It is not known whether the final decision was influenced by these people but the project did not go ahead.

As with other local inns, The King's Head was used for sales, auctions, etc. In 1805 a timber sale was announced and a sales catalogue was available at this pub. It was noted that the trees were on various farms in the area and close to the Surrey Iron Railway (recently opened). In this pre-steam train era perhaps an important consideration for anyone wishing to transport the timber. The following year catalogues were available here for the sale of stock for bankrupt calico printer Margaret Keatch. Also that year particulars were available here for the sale of farm land in Durnsford road which was intended to be used for building. At this time it has to be remembered that much of the area nearby was as yet undeveloped. Later that century the inn was used as a venue for property auctions.

In the late Victorian era there was quite a strong temperance movement in Wimbledon as elsewhere but it was ironic that in August 1887 the King's Head was chosen for a fete organised by the Hope of Merton Lodge, Original Order of Total Abstinence Sons of the Phoenix (How did they fit all that onto the membership card?) They did though use the field at the back rather than the pub itself.

In 1901 the landlord, Mr Busbridge, was called to an inquest after a woman died of alcohol poisoning. She had sent her 12-year-old daughter to the pub four times in one morning to buy rum and had apparently previously sold her children's boots and clothing as well as her own house to raise money for drink. The landlord protested that a publican had 'no right to ask questions of persons buying drink' and that the law did not forbid the sale of alcohol to children. The coroner, Mr Braxton Hicks, said that common sense did. The jury recommended that publicans should not sell alcohol to children and the coroner forwarded this recommendation to the Home Secretary. In August of that year Parliament passed into law the Intoxicating Liquors (Sale to Children) Act forbidding publicans from selling alcohol to children under the age of fourteen. It seems that this bill was already being looked at before Mr Braxton Hicks contacted the Home Secretary but this case may well have played a part in getting the bill through Parliament.

The King's Head was quite a substantial property. An entry in the 1838 rate book shows that there was a house, offices, a yard and garden plus a meadow and three cottages. The Wimbledon and Merton annual of 1906 states that the Dorking coach used to change horses here.

In his book Reminiscences of Old Merton (1925) W.H. Chamberlain talks of the coaching service from here to central London and that users of the service included local millionaire Richard Thornton, (once reputedly known as the richest man in England), and Sir Richard Hotham, (who lived at Merton Grove nearby and who was the founder of Bognor as a seaside resort). Others have asserted that Lord Nelson, who lived almost opposite the inn, used its coach services and may even have hired a carriage from here to take him on his final journey from Merton to Portsmouth and on to Trafalgar where he met his demise. Mr Chamberlain tells us that one of the coach drivers was a Mr George Hoath, a relative of his, though this presumably would have been much later, in the late nineteenth or even early twentieth century.

Chamberlain also mentions that next door to the inn was the smithy, run by a Mr Baylis who, apart from his usual work of a blacksmith, also performed duties as a veterinary surgeon.

The King's Head was also a stopping-off point for villagers 'beating the bounds' – a ceremony at which people from the parish of Wimbledon would walk round the entire parish boundary to remind children as well as their neighbours in Merton and other nearby parishes where the parish boundary line was. According to a local newspaper report in 1894 this ceremony was performed 'septennially' – i.e. every seven years – and that the participants lunched afterwards at the King's Head.

In an oral history project of the 1980s one elderly local remembered that there was once a large stage at the back of the pub in a garden area and shows were put on every Saturday night. The drivers from the bus garage next door had their own theatrical

King's Head, c. 1930

company and put on musical shows there. In the 1950s The King's Head was a jazz venue and in October 1956 the celebrated saxophonist Tubby Hayes played here. He had attended the nearby Rutlish School just a few years before.

The pub was bought on a lease by Young & Bainbridge in 1831 and they bought the freehold in 1899. It continued through the twentieth century and finally closed in 2004. There had been some opposition to the closure. CAMRA did not want to see another real ale pub closing and also pointed out that the building had some interesting architectural features. The Sutton Acoustic Music group regularly used the pub for concerts attracting large numbers of people and the local residents' group voiced objections to the closure. However, Young's did not feel it was attracting enough custom and unfortunately could not see a viable way of keeping it open.

COFFEE HOUSES

In the late Victorian era there was a strong and active local temperance movement which had had its first meeting in the Wimbledon Village club in 1868. Some people had tried to find alternatives to pubs for people to go to and thought coffee 'taverns' might be the answer. The Wimbledon Coffee Palace was at the corner of St George's Road but was outlasted by both the Alexandra and the South Western Hotel nearby. In the 1890s there were two coffee houses in Merton High Street, the Hope Coffee Palace, near Hardy Road and J.H. Raywood's coffee rooms next to the mission room by the Wandle. Both probably directly connected to the temperance movement.

MANSEL ARMS TAVERN (LATER SOUTH WESTERN HOTEL)

This pub began trading in 1855 when John Diaper was granted a licence in March. He had been working as head waiter at the Talbot hotel in Bradford and managed to save £200 (about £22,000 today) and borrow £200 from a friend with which to take out a mortgage on the pub.

The railway station had only opened in 1838 (next to the pub, on the west side of the bridge, not in its present position) and the Broadway and indeed the rest of Wimbledon was yet to be developed. Cows grazed in what was to be the Broadway and there was just a handful of houses nearby. The rest was fields. Businessmen who lived in the village would be driven down to the station in horse-drawn carriages to catch the train to Waterloo. The pub was therefore mainly there to serve the users of the new railway station. A 'railway tavern' had been first mooted in March 1853 when a Mr Wilson applied to Wandsworth magistrates but the application was refused as the 'house was not finished or rated.' A lease that was sold later though ran from 1852.

The pub did not start well. Within just over a year of its opening, landlord John Diaper was in the bankruptcy court in April 1856. The assignees failed to find anyone to take the pub over so in September of that year all the fixtures and fittings were auctioned off in the pub. Even the horse and cart were sold. It was concluded that the licensee had taken on the pub with too little capital. He had debts of £1,270 (almost £140,000 today) and assets of only £590.

On April 7, 1856 the pub had been advertised for sale along with two pairs of 'substantial brick-built semi-detached villa residences contiguous to the Wimbledon station.' It seems the owner of all these properties had gone bankrupt too.

Happily, the Mansel Arms survived this early setback. In January 1857 it was being advertised for sale again. It is described as a 'free licensed house with stabling, a large yard and a good supply of water.' Although we take the availability of water for granted now Wimbledon had only had a mains water supply for five years at that point, and many living on higher ground still had to rely on wells. The pub was also described as a 'railway hotel', another selling point for a potential buyer.

Strangely, another insolvent debtor, named Richard Wallace Pedder, whose various addresses included the Mansel Arms was in a newspaper dated August 8, 1857. Whether or not he was the next owner, we do not know.

The pub recovered though, and by 1858 was, like the Alexandra, a venue for inquests. On May 15 of that year the coroner here was told of the body of a young girl found near the railway lines. It was concluded that she had been thrown from a train. It had been discovered by men laying water pipes so it seems the provision of mains water was still not completed in this area despite having been begun in 1852.

By 1860 the pub seemed to be thriving and was being run by a Mr Meader. Taking advantage of the open land to the rear of the pub he was organising shooting parties. In November that year he advertised an event at which men could shoot for a 'fat pig' weighing 18 stone. The targets for the shooting were starlings. Prices are given for 'members' so it was already established as a club.

In December of that year the landlord organised another shooting party, this time for a 'fat ox'. It is mentioned that there are twenty members of the club.

Sadly, four years later, the landlord, Mr Meader was made bankrupt in December 1864 and all the stock was auctioned off at the pub. It consisted of: 'bar and coffee room fittings, pewter pots, measures, casks, stocks of wine, ale, porter, and numerous other effects'. However, it was back in business before too long and we find that in 1867 it was being run by a Gilbert Fownes.

What is remarkable about pubs of this era is how many different functions they fulfilled as well as being simply places to drink. In February 1861 there was a bad railway accident nearby and because one of the men was so badly injured that he couldn't be taken to a central London hospital, he was brought here to be attended to by a doctor. At the time there was no hospital in Wimbledon, the first, Wimbledon Cottage Hospital, was not to open until 1869. One of the other passengers injured in the accident was Dr Baly, assistant physician to Queen Victoria.

Another aspect of the pub's activities was that a carriage service was being run from here by a Mr James Berryman. This would have been convenient for people alighting from the train who lived in Wimbledon Village, and also for those visiting the National Rifle Association meetings on Wimbledon Common. In fact, in 1867, Mr Berryman was officially approved by the NRA as the sole agent for the conveyance of passengers to and from Wimbledon railway station after complaints had been made regarding opportunist drivers pitching for business and overcharging. We also find that in 1864 a 'riding master' by the name of Benjamin Blake was based here and was living at No.1 Mansel Villas, near to the pub.

In 1866 A French teacher named Le Page was returning home after giving a lesson at the house of Wimbledon engineer Joseph Bazalgette when he crossed the railway tracks to get to his platform and was hit by an express train. Bazalgette must have been seeing him off at the station as he witnessed the accident and gave evidence at the inquest held here. The previous year Bazalgette had seen the grand opening of the London sewage system he designed which was opened by the Prince of Wales. While the inquest was taking place the bodies of two workmen were brought into the pub who had been killed at the very same spot as Mr Le Page.

The pub also served as a venue for property and land sales and auctions, political meetings and court hearings.

In 1879 there was a very unfortunate accident here when someone left the pavement entrance to the cellar open and a passing postman fell down it. The postman, Mr Benjamin Morris, took out a summons against the landlord, William Silcock, who had not put a fence or handrail around the opening (health & safety is nothing new!). Mr Silcock was fined one pound and the postman was awarded £5 damages (over £1,250 today).

The pub seems to have become quite a substantial enterprise as in the 1881 census we find that living there as well as the owner, William Silcock and his wife and eight children there are also two barmen, a cook, a pot man and another servant described as a 'nurse'.

The name of the pub seems to have changed in the 1870s. The 1878 directory shows the new name though as late as 1894 a newspaper report mentions 'the Mansel Arms Hotel, now more familiarly known as the South-Western Hotel'. In many newspaper reports the original name was spelt 'Mansell'.

In December 1881 an inquest was begun here into one of the most notorious murder cases Wimbledon had seen. A doctor named George Henry Lamson had murdered his 18-year-old brother-in-law, Percy Malcolm John, in order to gain an inheritance. The court had assembled in a room at the pub, but the coroner, Mr Hall, decided it wasn't big enough to accommodate all the jury and witnesses and moved the proceedings to the nearby drill hall in St George's Road. The poisoning case eventually went to the Old Bailey and Lamson was hanged on April 18, 1882. (For the full story see Mysterious Wimbledon, published 1994.)

The South Western cropped up in the Wimbledon News dated April 7, 1900 when Wimbledon Hill restaurant Genoni's was applying for a drinks licence. The restaurant complained that when their customers wanted to order beer or wine they had to send a waiter over to the South Western for the drinks. The Swiss restaurant owner, Mr Clemente Genoni had managed to get a petition of 800 signatures from his customers in support of the appeal though the South Western pub, perhaps naturally, in view of the trade it was getting, opposed the application. The restaurant was granted a licence but on the conditions that the bar area was sealed off from the restaurant at the back, with no rear entry, and that alcohol was only served with meals.

In 1934 another Wimbledon Hill restaurant, Johnston's, applied for a renewal of its drinks licence and was opposed by the South Western and the Alexandra. It was pointed out to the magistrates that the restaurant customers could always have the drinks sent in from these pubs. In the end the licence was granted. It didn't seem to do the pubs any harm though as they continued to flourish long after the restaurant had gone. When the restaurant applied for a renewal again in 1937 the above two pubs were joined by the nearby Prince of Wales in opposition to it, though again the renewal went ahead subject to conditions similar to those that applied in 1900.

In the 1940s the pub was a regular haunt of someone who was to become a notorious double murderer and end up in the Chamber of Horrors at Madame Tussaud's. Neville Heath lived nearby in Merton Hall Road and was a regular at the 'South Western Hotel' as it was then known. He was friendly with the manager, Angus Bruce, and the two had socialised elsewhere. At that time of course no one knew what was to come when in 1946 Heath murdered and mutilated two women, one in a Notting Hill hotel, and another in Bournemouth. He was later hanged for the crimes. In another strange local twist, Heath went on a date that year with actress Moira Lister who had appeared in a couple of films made at nearby Merton Park film studios – one in 1945, just a year before she met Heath.

Robert James, whose father had taken the pub over in 1939, remembers them moving out during the Blitz. Perhaps this was just as well as in 1940 an anti-aircraft shell fell right outside the front of the pub. He remembers that stars working at Wimbledon Theatre, such as Tessie O'Shea, would come here, also a film producer from Merton Park studios. Through this connection he worked for a while as a 'clapper boy' on the Scotland Yard films and also on the Goons' Case of the Mukkinese Battle-Horn which were made there. He also said that in those days they had Saturday night dances at the Town Hall and that in the interval everyone would rush up to the pub for a drink.

The pub had a large public bar, a saloon bar on the right and a private bar at the front. No garden, but a big car park. This was before drink/driving laws of course! There was also a restaurant that started just before the war serving classic English fare such as Brown Windsor soup, meat and two veg, etc.

In October 1973 one of the barmen was arrested at the pub on burglary charges. Joseph Bailey was accused of stealing property worth £4,000 from houses in Somerset Road and Putney. He was remanded for medical and psychiatric reports.

In 1974 the Wimbledon News reported that although the pub had previously been threatened with demolition prior to redevelopment it had just obtained a five-year extension to its lease. The owners promptly spent £12,000 doing it up.

The South Western finally closed in November 1981 when the buildings opposite the station were knocked down for redevelopment. The Wimbledon News noted that the pub had been rebuilt in 1891 and current owners Ind Coope had only eighteen months previously spent £23,000 refurbishing the place.

PUBS AS ESTATE AGENTS

When property was being sold in the Victorian era, auctioneers would use local pubs in which to advertise details. An advert of 1866 shows two semi-detached houses in Southey Road for sale with particulars available at The White Hart, Dog & Fox, Mansel Arms and Freemason's Arms (they meant the Freeman Arms, former name of the Broadway pub). The rental value of these ten-roomed houses was £110 a year. Pubs were also used for the sale of land and during the time the town was being built there was much land being sold locally.

MARQUIS OF LORNE

This pub was in Haydon's Road by 1880 when being run by Samuel Tebbut who had run the Raynes Park Tavern in 1874. It was therefore the third pub to open in Haydon's Road in fifty years, being preceded by the Horse & Groom (by 1838) and the British Queen (1860). Several other small beer shops had already opened in the roads off Haydon's Road too so the local population, which was still expanding, had plenty of choice of drinking venues.

In the 1970s the pub acquired something of a Cockney flavour when it was being run by Alf and Sadie who had been born in the East End. On Friday, Saturday and Sunday nights they had busker 'Old Ruby' (a man) playing Cockney favourites such as Knees Up Mother Brown and My Old Man on the banjo or squeeze box. It was also a big favourite with local policemen and one told of how even coppers from Scotland Yard would come here for the atmosphere. In those days the beer was cheap too – a pint of light and bitter there was 18p.

In 2007 the pub lost its licence as the Wimbledon Guardian reported that it had been branded by police as 'a meeting place for armed gangs, and a hub for criminal activity and drug dealing.'

In the eleven months before its licence was lost the police had received 75 intelligence reports highlighting concerns about the pub. These included reports of a planned fight between rival gangs and weapons such as machetes, knives, an air rifle and a crossbow were found on the premises as well as class A and C drugs.

It was announced in November 2019 that the pub would be converted into six flats with the original front and side fascias being retained.

PERSEVERANCE

This was one of the small beer shops in the Haydon's Road area in the 1860s but seems to have been short-lived. Edward Toomes had been a greengrocer and fishmonger in 1855, then a 'beer retailer' from 1862–66 and was finally running this pub in 1867 in Haydon's Lane (former name of Haydon's Road). Unfortunately, no street number is given. It seems to have gone by 1871 (*see* White Hart).

NORTH, EAST AND SOUTH ROADS

These three roads, just off Haydon's Road had been the first part of 'New Wimbledon' to be developed. By 1974 though Merton Council decided it was time to redevelop the area, declaring hundreds of houses 'unfit'. Local pub owners however, were against this, arguing that the properties could simply be refurbished. The landlords of the Horse and Groom, Marquis of Lorne and White Hart all protested though perhaps they were exercised too by the fact that there were plans to build a new pub at the corner of Haydon's Road and All Saints Road and possibly a second one at the corner of Haydon's Road and Cowper Road. These new pubs never materialized and the three existing pubs continued for varying lengths of time.

Marquis of Lorne

Plasterers Arms

PLASTERERS ARMS

Another small beer shop in the same area, this time in South Road. The owner, James Clarke, had been running a beer shop since 1865 but the name Plasterers Arms does not appear until 1881. Amazingly, it lasted until 1961, though in 1924 things had not been looking good for this and some other small pubs in the area. At the annual licensing sessions it was announced that all the licences in the division would be renewed except those for the Plasterers Arms, as well as those for the Duke of Cambridge and the White Hart, which were both in nearby North Road. The decisions on these were to be deferred. Perhaps the magistrates were wondering why this small area needed so many pubs and beer shops, not to mention off-licences.

When this pub did close though it effectively gave birth to a new pub in Kingston Road, the Emma Hamilton, which could not open until a licence became available.

TIME GENTLEMEN PLEASE

In February 1924 the annual licensing sessions took place at the police court in Wimbledon. Presided over by Mr Percy H. Clarke, the justices included the wonderfully named Lieutenant-General Sir Launcelotte Gubbins. The Christian Social Council put forward the suggestion that Sunday closing time should be 9.00 pm rather than the then current 10.00 pm. This was opposed by the South West London Licensed Victuallers Society. The vicar of Wimbledon claimed that large numbers of children were being left outside pubs while their mothers were inside. He produced statistics showing that on one Sunday evening 94 children were seen outside pubs between 9.00 and 10.00 pm. Sub-divisional police Inspector Cavendish said he had seen no evidence of children being left outside pubs at night. A decision on opening times was adjourned.

PLOUGH (ALSO KNOWN AS PLOW & HARROW)

One of the oldest pubs in Wimbledon, the Plough, which gave its name to Plough Lane in which it stood, was there from at least 1721 when it was being run by William Gravott. A victuallers list of 1727 shows that the landlord then was James Pether.

When residents of 18th century Wandsworth were beating the bounds in this area where the parishes of Wimbledon and Wandsworth met, the Plough was used as a refreshment stop.

We sometimes only hear about past pubs when they have been in trouble with the law. In 1846 the landlady, Jane Woodruff, who had been running the place for twenty-two years was taken to court for opening the pub before 1.00 pm on a Sunday. In 1887 landlord John Edward Smith was also summonsed for opening the pub on a Sunday morning. Interestingly, the publican managed to excuse himself by saying that two of the three men drinking in the pub were travelling from Camberwell which apparently gave him dispensation from prosecution. The third man claimed that he had merely gone there to fetch some brandy for his sick wife. Surprisingly, the case was dropped.

In 1898 it was the pub's landlady, Jessie Blackmore, who was the victim of a crime here. Two men were accused of stealing 47 packets of tobacco and five bottles of spirits. They were also charged with breaking *out* of the pub! They claimed they had been accidentally locked in the night before and had to break out in the morning. Only one of the men was convicted, and given what the bench called a 'light sentence' of three months in prison.

In 1924 a question came up at the annual licensing sessions about people from Wandsworth coming 'over the border' to the Plough in Wimbledon to enjoy an extra hour's drinking as the pub closed at 10.00 pm on a Sunday as opposed to the 9.00 pm closing time of the Wandsworth pubs. The drinkers wouldn't have had far to come as just across the road were the White Lion (later the Hare & Hounds) and the Corner Pin (both in Summerstown).

The road which the pub gave its name to didn't exist until the 19th century when the copper works which were based there extended a road running through their grounds down to Garratt Lane in the 1840s. The area was otherwise undeveloped with fields on either side. One of those fields, with rather swampy ground, was used as a rubbish dump though it was later put to good use by Wimbledon Football Club which took it over as their home ground just before the First World War.

The many functions of a pub have been mentioned elsewhere in this book, but another one, that of betting shop, has not, partly because betting on the horses away from the racetrack was illegal before 1961 and therefore any betting in pubs was clandestine. Before betting shops were legalised it was not uncommon for bookies' runners to be collecting bets on street corners and in pubs – often in the toilets away from prying eyes. In June 1957 the Plough was raided by police when they had been tipped off that betting was taking place on the premises. They had been watching the pub for a week and seen betting take place, with the runner laying off bets in the public telephone box outside. In court it was decided that the landlord knew nothing about the betting and as the defendant was an old soldier living on a pension with no previous convictions he was just given a £5 fine plus costs.

The pub closed in 2006 and in 2010 the building was taken over by a tile company. Interestingly, the business address was The Plough, Plough Lane rather than simply a street number.

It was reported in December 2020 that the building will become a McDonald's.

The Plough

ST GEORGE

This was another of the small beer shops that sprang up just off Haydon's Road in the late Victorian era. It was in South Road by 1887 when it was being run by Henry Irons. It does not appear to have lasted long; the last entry in local directories was 1903 and Mr Irons had been the sole owner throughout the pub's existence.

WHITE HART

Yet another one of these small beer shops as above. Edward Toomes had been running the Perseverance in Haydon's Road (*see separate entry*) since 1867 but by 1871 he was in North Road running this pub with his wife Elizabeth. Both were 60 years old. Also living there were his son, also Edward, a carpenter, aged 20 and daughter Mary Ann, aged 17. By 1881 it was being run by Frederick Baldwin. According to the census of that year he was a painter and beer house keeper. The pub lasted a lot longer than some of the other small beer shops in this area though in 1924 its licence was not automatically renewed as most others were in the area apart from the Duke of Cambridge and the Plasterers Arms nearby.

The pub finally closed in 1980 so had lasted for more than a century. A Wimbledon News reporter visited there in 1984 and found the sorry sight of the abandoned pub inhabited only by rats. The building had also been the target of young arsonists. The British Legion had applied for planning permission to take it over as their clubhouse but discussions with the Charrington brewery were still in progress at that time and presumably came to nothing.

It was a shame that it ended this way as the picture of the pub below from around 1914 shows the regulars, some in army uniform, standing outside what would then have been a popular community pub. The names lives on however, in the group of houses in North Road which are named White Hart Lodge.

The White Hart, North Road, Wimbledon

PUBS OF 20TH AND 21ST CENTURY ORIGIN

In the mid-1990s there was a sudden rash of new pubs opening up in Wimbledon but there was quite a bit of opposition, partly from those who felt we needed more shops in the town centre rather than more pubs, and partly from those who were concerned about anti-social behaviour. There was of course also opposition from the other, already established, pubs such as The Broadway and The Prince of Wales as well as JJ's wine bar who felt there was no need for additional pubs that would affect their trade. In February 1995 though, permission was granted for the opening of what were to be the Wibbas Down by the theatre and Chumley's on the corner of Kings Road. The go-ahead for what was to become the Hand & Racquet on Wimbledon Hill had already been given the previous month – again despite opposition, and approval for the old Barclays Bank building to be converted into a branch of the All Bar One pub chain had been granted in 1994. Elys department store pointed out that there were now more pubs and restaurants in the area than shops. In May 1996 the Wimbledon News quipped: 'Another new pub sparks fears for Wimbledon's lager-than-life town centre'.

So, here are the modern pubs, which naturally do not have much history and despite being relatively recent additions to the area, not all have even survived as far as 2021.

ALL BAR ONE

A modern pub at the bottom of Wimbledon Hill housed in the old bank building. Opened 1995.

BATSFORD ARMS

Most people could be forgiven for never having heard of this pub. It was rather exclusive, being the home supporters bar under the South stand at Wimbledon Football Club in Plough Lane. It opened in 1972 and closed in 1985 when the South stand was condemned.

CAVERN

Is it a coincidence that the Cavern in Coombe Lane, Raynes Park opened in 1991, the same year that the famous Cavern club in Liverpool reopened? As the name implies, the emphasis is on rock music and apart from rock you can hear blues, tribute bands and the occasional big name such as Mud.

EDWARD RAYNE

This Wetherspoons pub opened in September 2006 just near Raynes Park station and was housed in an old branch of the Co-op. When it opened the manager was quoted as saying that they hoped to attract a 'classier clientele'. It was also a non-smoking pub almost a year before the official nationwide smoking ban came into force in July 2007. In mid-2021 it is closed and boarded up. It is not known if it will reopen as a pub.

Allen Batsford outside the pub named after him

HAND AND RACQUET

Another modern pub which opened in 1995, housed in an old branch of Boots in Wimbledon Hill Road. Was known for a while as The Hogshead.

KING LEOPOLD

This pub opened in Leopold Road in 1993 in what was formerly a restaurant. A Cypriot had opened a restaurant/wine bar here in 1989 but decided to convert it to a pub as there was no other pub nearby. It was a free house but mainly served Young's beer with some guest ales. It seems to have gone back to restaurant use by 1999.

OLD FRIZZLE

This pub in Wimbledon Broadway was originally known as Chumley's when it was
opened in 1995 by Regent Inns before becoming Walkabout, one of a chain of
Australian bars, then Billabong. It is now owned by a pub chain called Livelyhood
and boasts a ceiling made from part of an old squash court. In 2005 when it was still
the Walkabout bar staff were given T shirts to wear bearing the slogan 'No dancing'.
This was because the pub did not have a public entertainment licence and Merton
Council was investigating whether it was flouting its licence conditions.

O'NEILL'S

One of an Irish-themed pub chain run by Mitchell and Butler. Opened in 1996 and
housed in what was the Notting Hill Housing Trust charity shop in Wimbledon
Broadway. According to the Wimbledon News of May 3, 1996 the pub aimed to
'capture the evolution of the Irish bar from its roots as a shop, reflecting the
eccentricity of Irish pubs.' A reporter from the Wimbledon Guardian claimed in 2010
that the pub served the 'finest pint of Guinness in Wimbledon'.

SPORTSMAN

A short-lived pub, but remembered with affection by fans of Wimbledon FC as it was in Durnsford Road right outside their Plough Lane ground. The building was originally the supporters' clubhouse but was turned into a pub, run by Young's brewery, in 1971 in order to bring more money into the club. It closed in 1998 when the Plough Lane ground closed. In 1957 when the supporters wanted a club house then Chairman Sydney Black said that if they could raise £750.00 he would build them a club house. They actually raised £1,200.00 and the building was put up the following year at a cost of £8,000.00. There was also a 'Dons' Bar' at the back of the North stand which became the Wimbledon Supporters' Club base when the Sportsman became a fully-fledged public house open to the public. In addition to this there was Nelson's nightclub, also part of the North stand which ran WSC functions in the 1970s and raised more funds for the club than the gate receipts. The Dons returned to Plough Lane in their new stadium in 2021 and there are plans to open a new pub, called The Phoenix, in autumn 2021. Public access from Coppermill Lane.

TOWNHOUSE

Yet another pub that opened up in the 1990s, but unlike some of the others, has not survived till today. It was at the bottom of Wimbledon Hill near the junction of Worple Road from around 1992 and had previously been a Berni Inn. It had a car park at the back which was used as a drinking area in the summer.

WIBBAS DOWN

Opened in 1995 this Wetherspoon's pub is the largest in Wimbledon, having entrances in Gladstone Road and Russell Road. It was formerly a branch of Tesco.

THE PUB NAMES

There are many reasons for which a pub acquires its name. It could be related to a historical event or person, local or national, it could be an attempt to appeal to a particular clientele, it could be humorous, or in some cases there appears to be no particular reason at all for the chosen name. With some of the modern pubs the name is simply the same as all the other pubs in the chain to which it belongs.

Occasionally though, a pub's name becomes part of the fabric of the area when a road is named after it. Even when the pub has long ceased to exist its memory will be kept alive in the road name, as with Plough Lane – which also became a metonym for Wimbledon FC's ground.

So here are the stories behind those names.

ALEXANDRA

Princess Alexandra of Denmark married Albert, Prince of Wales (later Edward VII) on March 10, 1863 in St George's chapel, Windsor Castle. It was as a result of this that the Alexandra and other local pubs acquired names relating to the royal couple. Bertie's wine bar in the basement of the Prince of Wales is of course named after Albert, Prince of Wales.

ALL BAR ONE

This is the name for all pubs in this chain and has no special significance.

BATSFORD ARMS

Allen Batsford was manager of Wimbledon FC from 1974 to 1977 and in that short time took them to three consecutive league titles and in 1977 entry to the Football League.

BAY TREE

It is far from certain whether this establishment ever was a pub as it was usually described as a temperance hotel, but 'Bay Tree' is not an uncommon pub name and seems to have no local significance.

BILLABONG

When Walkabout closed the pub was given this name for a while presumably in an attempt to continue the Australian theme.

BRITANNIA

Clearly a patriotic name, but could it have been inspired by a ship of that name? Many pubs in Merton have had names with nautical connections, particularly after Lord Nelson's many naval successes.

BRITISH QUEEN

When this pub began in 1860 the monarch was of course Queen Victoria, so another patriotic name.

BROADWAY ARMS/HOTEL

Clearly named after the road in which it stood, this pub had previously been called The Freeman Arms when that part of the road was still called Merton Road rather than The Broadway.

CAVERN

There was once a quite well-known club in Liverpool called The Cavern. This is a music venue so what better name?

CHUMLEY'S

Owner Regent Inns had another Chumley's in Reading so there seems to be no local significance for this name.

DUKE OF CAMBRIDGE

Probably named after Prince George, who became Duke of Cambridge in 1850. After he died in 1904 the title was not to be used again until 2011 when it was given to Prince William.

DUKE OF EDINBURGH

In 1866 the title Duke of Edinburgh had not been in use for more than a century but then Queen Victoria revived it to be used by her son Prince Alfred. It would therefore have been in the minds of people searching for a new name for this pub which began in 1869. Also, the Duke of Edinburgh himself had visited the National Rifle Association meeting on Wimbledon Common in August 1868.

EDWARD RAYNE

Named of course after the landowner who gave his name to Raynes Park. Strictly speaking, the pub isn't in Raynes Park, which is the area south of the railway line, but in Cottenham Park.

FREEMAN ARMS

There has been a suggestion that this name could be connected with freemasonry, but as there are other pubs in Britain named The Freemasons' Arms that idea can probably be discounted. The other suggestion was that the pub had been set up by a freeman of the City of London, but there is no record of the first owner having received this honour. Perhaps the original owner, who had worked for the landlord at the Rose and Crown, was celebrating the fact that he was now running his own pub.

GARDEN SHED

The Horse and Groom, the oldest surviving pub in Wimbledon outside the Village, had its name changed a few years ago to the Garden Shed. The owners held an online poll and this was the name chosen by the public. It is not clear whether this was chosen from a list of limited options but the name seems to have no special significance and it is a mystery as to why the name needed to be changed when the Horse & Groom name had been in use for the best part of two centuries. But as it is one of the only pubs left in that area when so many have gone perhaps we should be glad that it has survived at all – whatever the name.

HAND & RACQUET

A clear reference to the All England tennis club though until 2007 there used to be another Hand & Racquet pub in London – in Whitcomb Street WC2 which commemorated a royal tennis court that was nearby in Whitehall and was used by Charles II.

HAYDON'S

The British Queen was renamed Haydon's in the 1990s, presumably in an attempt to give it a more contemporary feel. What may not have been realised is that the name originally came from an 18th century landowner by the name of George Heydon who had a farm here in the 1760s and 1770s and after whom the road was named.

HOGSHEAD

The Hand & Racquet's name was changed to Hogshead during the 1990s but when the Hogshead chain was rebranded it reverted to its original name.

HORSE & GROOM

A common pub name, but when this pub opened in Haydon's Road in the 1830s the surrounding area was mainly farmland with few buildings so it was probably intended to appeal to members of the then rural community.

JOINERS ARMS

Pub owners were often aiming for a specific clientele with their choice of name, and with these small beer shops the clientele would often be working men like themselves. Many tradesmen ran a small pub as a sideline. The owner in this case was a carpenter.

JUNCTION TAVERN

A reference to the railway junction nearby, even though the pub preceded the station.

KING LEOPOLD ARMS

Why was this Wimbledon pub named after the nineteenth century King of the Belgians? Probably by mistake. Leopold Road was named after Arthur, Duke of Connaught's brother Leopold. Both men were friends of John Augustus Beaumont, landowner and developer of Wimbledon Park and this part of Wimbledon. King Leopold had been a maternal uncle of Queen Victoria.

KING'S HEAD

One of the commonest pub names and one which of course appeals to people's patriotism. If the claim of 1496 as the pub's start date is true the king in question would have been Henry VII, first of the Tudor monarchs. In fact, a photo from the 1980s shows Henry VII on a sign on the pub wall.

MANSEL TAVERN

The Mansel family owned land in Wimbledon, including some at the foot of Wimbledon Hill. They also gave their name to nearby Mansel Road.

MARQUIS OF LORNE

This pub could have been called The John George Edward Henry Douglas Sutherland Campbell, 9th Duke of Argyll, KG, KT, GCMG, GCVO, VD, PC. Thankfully, the owners decided instead to adopt his courtesy title The Marquis of Lorne which he used from 1847 onwards. He was Governor General of Canada from 1878 to 1883 and several places there are named after him. He would therefore have been very much in the public eye when this pub opened in 1880.

OLD FRIZZLE

This refers to an ace of spades playing card that had been stamped to show that duty had been paid on an item.

O'NEILL'S

A generic name for this Irish-themed pub chain.

PERSEVERANCE

It is said that this not uncommon pub name can sometimes be chosen by a person who has waited a long time to gain his drinks licence. This could be the case here as the owner, Edward Toomes, was listed in local directories as a 'beer retailer' from 1862–66 and in 1867 he is shown as running The Perseverance in 'Haydon's Lane' (former name of Haydon's Road), possibly with a full licence so it may be that the name of the pub is a reference to his long wait to become a pub owner.

PLASTERERS ARMS

As with the Joiners Arms, this little beer shop was unashamedly aiming directly at the working men who lived in the small houses nearby.

PLOUGH/PLOW & HARROW

With farmland nearby and few houses it would have made sense to aim this pub directly at the agricultural workers who would have been the inn's main customers in the 18th century. The harrow is a farming tool for smoothing out soil.

PRINCE OF WALES

Another pub name inspired by that royal wedding in 1863 (*see* Alexandra). The wedding was also the inspiration for the King of Denmark pub which stood in the Ridgway until a few years ago as Alexandra was daughter of the King of Denmark. Another reason for the pub being so named is that in July 1863 the Prince of Wales visited the National Rifle Association meeting on Wimbledon Common and came again in 1864 and 1866 so perhaps that would have been fresh in the minds of those naming the pub.

RAYNES PARK HOTEL/TAVERN

As with the Edward Rayne, this pub is not actually in Raynes Park, but Cottenham Park, though most people these days call the whole area, both north and south of the railway, Raynes Park.

SOUTH WESTERN HOTEL

Another railway connection as this pub, formerly the Mansel Arms/Tavern, was next to the original Wimbledon station through which the south western trains ran.

SPORTSMAN

Being virtually attached to the old Wimbledon FC ground it is perhaps not surprising that it was given this name, though several others were considered, including The Nod Inn and The Corner Post. There was also some talk of honouring former chairman Sydney Black in the pub's name but this was decided against as his family had been involved with the temperance movement. Eventually the name Wibbandune (an old name for Wimbledon) was chosen, before being changed to The Sportsman a year later due to its unpopularity with fans. Interestingly, there was a local cricket team named Wibbandune (est. 1936, and still playing) and Wibbandune is also the name of the home ground of Colliers Wood United FC today.

ST GEORGE

Simple patriotism presumably for the patron saint of England.

SULTAN

Said to be named after a racehorse of that name, though the pub, established by 1868, was named quite a long time after the heyday of this particular stallion, which had been in the 1820s.

TOWNHOUSE

A rather uninspired bit of punning perhaps.

WALKABOUT

Just one of many identically named pubs in this chain.

WHITE HART

A very common pub name, the sign of which originally depicted the heraldic symbol of Richard II, though the name later became almost a generic name for a pub.

WIBBANDUNE

See 'Sportsman'.

WIBBAS DOWN

Wetherspoons pubs will often be named in accordance with some local personality, history or tradition and the name of this one comes from an early spelling of the name of Wimbledon, which has sometimes been given as Wibbandune (*see* The Sportsman above).

WOODMAN

When this pub first opened its doors it was surrounded by woodland and farmland with barely a building in sight – apart from the nearby cottage of the woodman who looked after the forest. A real reminder then of the rural area this was just 150 years ago.

ACKNOWLEDGEMENTS

British Newspaper Archive
Sarah Gould (Merton local studies library)
Tony Hedger and Geoff Strawbridge (CAMRA)
Matthew Hillier
Robert James
Steve Lock (book layout)
John Lynch at WISH (www.wimbledoninsportinghistory.com)
Surrey Record Office
Charles Toase
The Wimbledon Society

PHOTOGRAPHS/PICTURES

Alexandra – Young's brewery
Batsford Arms – John Lynch at WISH
British Queen – Merton Library Service
Duke of Edinburgh – John Innes Society
Freeman Arms – Historic England Archives
Hartfield Road off licence – author's own collection
Horse & Groom – taken by author
Junction Tavern – Merton Library Service
King's Head – author's own collection
Leopold Arms – Chris Matuszek/Wimbledon News
Lord Palmerston sign – taken by author
Marquis of Lorne – Merton Library Service
Plasterers Arms – Merton Library Service
Plough – Merton Library Service
Prince of Wales – author's own collection
Raynes Park Hotel – author's own collection
Sportsman – Merton Library Service
South Western Hotel – Patrick Loobey
Sultan – taken by author
White Hart – The Lost Pubs Project
Woodman – author's own collection
Cover painting of the Alexandra by Malcolm Nash
Back cover photo – Merton Library Service

BIBLIOGRAPHY

A–Z of Wimbledon – Charles Toase
Historic Wimbledon – Richard Milward
Mysterious Wimbledon – Ruth Murphy and Clive Whichelow
More Mysterious Wimbledon – Ruth Murphy and Clive Whichelow
Raynes Park, A Social History – E.M. Jowett
Reminiscences of Old Merton – W.H. Chamberlain
Safe as Houses – Norman Plastow